ZEN AND THE ART OF ADMIN TASKS

ZEN AND THE ART OF ADMIN TASKS

WRITTEN BY
NIC DE CASTRO
NATHAN PETTIJOHN

LIONCREST
PUBLISHING

ZEN AND THE ART OF ADMIN TASKS

ISBN   978-1-5445-1162-7 *Paperback*
        978-1-5445-1161-0 *Ebook*

CONTENTS

WHY WE WROTE
THIS BOOK

"Time is the coin of your life. It is the only coin you have, and only you can determine how it will be spent. Be careful lest you let other people spend it for you."
– CARL SANDBURG

Imagine any high-powered, wheeling-and-dealing CEO, and rest assured they have an administrative assistant helping to coordinate all the logistics that go into their busy schedules. When utilized properly, admins are a crucial part of maintaining a well-operating schedule and flow of communication. Meanwhile, entrepreneurs who don't delegate, and instead try handling every aspect of their business themselves, are rarely successful in scaling or managing all of their relationships. Sooner or later, something will slip between the cracks.

If you are spending 30% of your time on administrative tasks, that's time you aren't focused on the big picture. A 2016 study of 1,000 white-collar workers in the United States found that, "We spend an average of 4.1 hours checking our work email each day. That's 20.5 hours each week, more than 1,000 hours each year, more than *47,000 hours* over a career." On top of that, 79% of those interviewed said they check their work email while on vacation.

We know the power of quick and concise communication. This book is designed to help make communication smoother, not more complicated. Consider the following example.

We recently took a trip to Cuba with a group of our friends. While there, we had infrequent access to internet service, but neither of us set up an out-of-office reply that might give our clients pause. Instead, our admin (yes, we both have the same admin) was responding quickly to emails "as Nic" or "as Nate" and responses were coming in as though both of our businesses were operating as usual.

We were also able to glance at Todoist, our task management app, and see multiple projects being delegated by our admin, with different pieces of work being completed by freelancers according to a structured workflow. Because we know how to delegate and make efficient use of our admin, we were able to take a vacation almost entirely off-grid while our businesses kept running smoothly back home.

Now here's an example from the other side of the spectrum. One of our friends is a founder of a well-backed startup. He would stress over not having Internet access while we were in Cuba, and as soon as he did get Internet access he would spend an hour frantically responding to emails, and many of his responses were late.

We wrote this short book as a way to empower more people to focus on what's really important to them, in life and in their businesses. After all, it's in those moments when you're not buried in menial tasks that flashes of genius and creativity hit you. We like to call those moments "whitespace," and we believe that giving yourself as much whitespace as possible will enable you to have more of these sparks of creativity that will transform your work and life.

We didn't invent these principles. Fortune 500 CEOs have known the power of the admin for decades. Others, like Tim Ferriss, set the stage for us with his runaway bestseller *The 4-Hour Work Week*. It is our goal to make the categories of rules and processes in this short book simple enough for a reader to copy and paste them, with minor adjustments in order to make them specific to their own business.

Technology enables us with tools we can use to either make us more or less productive, but they are just tools. It is how we implement and use these tools that really matters. In his treatise titled *On the Equilibrium of Planes,* Greek mathematician Archimedes gave an explanation for the principles involved in using a lever. Today, people speak about leverage as though it is a strategy or tactic, but it is not. Leverage is a tool.

WHO THIS BOOK IS FOR

"Give me a lever long enough and a fulcrum on which to place it, and I shall move the world."
– ARCHIMEDES

This book is for you if:

- You own a small business but still manage your own email and scheduling
- You run sales for an organization but still personally respond to specific intros and leads and update your own CRM
- You are an entrepreneur (or VP or C-level executive) that gets easily distracted by your inbox instead of focusing on the big picture

Our goal is to provide an easy process to copy-and-paste where you can literally download this book, hire a virtual admin off a site like UpWork, and have your inbox and calendar delegated all in one day. You could even do it all in one sitting. This book is meant to be read in the span of an hour and immediately implemented.

Many entrepreneurs we have spoken to about this system immediately resist and push back. They'll says something like, "It sounds great in theory, but no admin could handle *my* inbox. I have to do it myself."

Oh really? Your inbox is more demanding, sensitive, and important than the general counsel for ExxonMobil? Or the CEO of Walmart? Because both of those people leverage admins in the same manner. We have news for you: your inbox is not a special snowflake that can't be processed with this system.

Another reaction we hear often is entrepreneurs who say they need someone working with them in person, usually because they have the idea that working in person together is somehow more effective. Working remotely can be just as, if not more, effective. If you doubt this fact, read the book *ReWork* by David Heinemeier Hansson and Jason Fried, about how they built and grew Basecamp with a tiny, remote team. The psychological benefits of seeing someone physically working in your office or their being available for you to make them wash your car on a whim or get your groceries or whatever—isn't worth it. Trust us.

Why does this book cover only your email and calendar? Because your inbox is where a majority of your tasks, projects, and time commitments come into your work queue. While there are always more tasks and processes to delegate, getting you away from managing your own email and calendar is essential if you are going to embrace these principles.

You do not need to pay $3,000 or more per month for a full-time employee to take over your inbox and calendar. As mentioned above, we share an admin between us, and we each pay her around 8 hours a week at a rate of $16 per hour. Nate also found his data entry person on UpWork. He was able to hire someone with good references who was available to meet in person occasionally—and who only cost $25 per hour. Anyone either of us hires has to sign a very specific NDA. Our clients are made aware of the organizational chart changes and have visibility into what we are doing. Some big corporations may not allow delegating your admin work to outside resources, so check with your boss or clients if you're unsure.

This book is not for everyone. You decide how valuable your time is, and whether doing 5-20 hours per week of admin work is an effective use of your time. We're betting it's not. Instead, document, delegate and automate as much as you can, and then you can start enjoying that whitespace that encourages breakthroughs.

WHAT THIS BOOK IS FOR

If you're still reading this, it means you're serious about taking your ideas, your business, and your time to the next level. You're ready to become truly productive, and do away once and for all with the repetition and exhaustion of time-consuming administrative tasks. It's time for the admin-automation revolution, and you want to be at the head of the curve.

In this book, we'll take you step by step through the processes that we've adopted to make our businesses run smoothly, optimizing our day-to-day for maximum effectiveness, maximum creativity, and minimum administrative fuss.

This is a no-nonsense, straightforward tactical guide. The processes you read about here will be actionable today, and you'll see concrete improvements in your workflow tomorrow. By setting up these systems, your business will be able to pass even the "hit-by-a-bus" resilience test. Your inbox, schedule, and client database will all continue to function as usual, even if you are suddenly indisposed (whether due to a bus crash or not).

Quality administrative work is a foundation for business success, but it is not where true, exponential value is added. It's hygiene. When you free yourself from admin tasks, you free yourself to pursue real value and growth. Now let's get started.

CHOOSING YOUR ADMIN

An important part of this system is choosing the right admin for your needs. We have had businesses over the years where we've tried offshore outsourcing to India or the Philippines. Hiring someone offshore does have its merits depending on the needs of the business, but for the purposes of this book we believe that choosing a localized admin is the right move.

As mentioned, we live in NYC and LA and we share the same admin who lives on the east coast of Florida. If you're based in the US, having an admin based on the east coast is ideal. They'll be at work at least as early as you if you're also located in the Eastern time zone. And they'll be at work hours before you if you're located in CST/MST/PST.

This means you're already responding to emails before your clients even get out of bed!

Nic originally found our admin through posting a job description on UpWork. We've included the original UpWork job posting that Nic used for reference in the appendix. He immediately had responses to his posting and scheduled video chats with select candidates. Nic actually hired the first person he interviewed. We believe this is because of the settings that he had selected on UpWork, which provided for a highly qualified set of candidates.

We have weekly calls with our admin to recap the week and go through emails, invites, and processes to continually improve and refine the system. New items arise and you have to add them to the rules. To do this, we simply have each of our rules saved as shared documents on Google Docs and we can edit them as evolving documents. We suggest that you copy and paste our rules in the following pages, and add them to a shared doc for your admin and then adjust as new processes come up. Start here, then continue to refine based on your specific needs.

Hire someone with a positive, friendly attitude and solid work ethic. Look for an admin with whom you feel a comfortable amount of trust based on their references, experience, and demeanor. Our admin has signed additional disclosure paperwork in order to have visibility on certain high priority accounts. Depending on the type of industry you're in, you may be required to hire someone in-house full-time to handle administrative work. If that's the case, you can still use these same rules and processes to immediately offload tasks in an efficient way.

Lastly, realize that there will be a ramp up period when your admin first starts where small mistakes might be made and rules will need tweaking. It's inevitable that something will not be done exactly as you would have done it yourself. That's okay. When it happens, simply refine the processes and rules and set times to go through each error and what should be done differently. Of course, if mistakes are occurring frequently you may need to consider other candidates. But if you do a thorough enough job in the interview stage you will have a smart and dependable admin that will make a proactive effort to improve workflow and correct mistakes.

THE TOOLS

Before beginning the automation process, it's fundamental to gather your arsenal of tools. Consider this section of the book your cheat sheet. We have tried and tested the full range of products, and found these tools and services to be most useful for step one of outsourcing and automating administrative work.

In the following chapters, we'll go into detail about how to make the best use of these tools.

1. **G Suite**
   A. **Gmail:** We use Gmail for both internal and external communication.
   B. **Google Calendar:** We use GCal for all scheduling tasks.

c. **Google Documents:** We create and manage all documents in Google Docs.

2. **UberConference:** We use this conference calling solution for all virtual meetings.

3. **Voicera:** This AI assistant (Eva) listens to all virtual meetings, creates transcripts, and notes down keywords from our conversations.

4. **Salesforce** & **Nimble:** We use these CRM's to update our contacts and pipelines (Nic uses Salesforce, Nate uses Nimble). We also create template emails within here and we are able to track email opens and link clicks.

5. **Connectifier:** We use this service to track down emails for contacts.

6. **ToDoist:** This collaborative task manager app allows us to keep track of what our team is working on.

7. **CrystalKnows, Detective:** We use these tools to prepare before meetings. Easily sync them with your Gmail and calendar to get insights on people and companies you are about to meet with.

8. **Boomerang (Chrome Extension):** This simple email scheduling tool is how we schedule emails to send at a later date.

9. **Loom (Chrome Extension):** We use this tool to record our screens when performing tasks that will need to be repeated in the future. Any new hires can refer to Loom folders on each individual process, allowing

onboarding without having to explain one process more than once.

10. **Upwork:** We use Upwork to find and hire admin or remote talent. There are plenty of similar sites, but hiring a reliable virtual admin is crucial so do your homework and hire someone with good references.

11. **Good old-fashioned mobile phone:** We use phone calls and text messages for urgent matters only.

In our appendix, you'll find a list of these tools with spaces for you to fill in your usernames and passwords, so you can easily distribute this information amongst your team and your administrator(s).

EMAIL RULES

Email is where nearly all work enters our world. Without outsourcing and automation, email can swallow you whole. Open your inbox and before you know it half the day is gone. Just by outsourcing email you'll save hours every day.

Here's the system we've created to streamline our administrative email tasks. By creating these clear rules, your admin can essentially automate his or her approach to your inboxes, allowing for fast response times, minimal hassle, and no missed opportunities.

Here are the guidelines we implement for our inboxes. Our admin follows these rules when processing our inboxes on our behalf. You can add to this list as you encounter new types of emails and create rules for those types of emails. You will note that these rules refer to 'Nate': simply substitute 'Nate' for your own name, and pass these rules on to whoever manages your inbox.

We suggest that right before you start this process, you let 100 or so unread work emails build up in your inbox. That way on day one, you can go through and process them with your admin and show them how you'd respond to and categorize each email. Or you can record yourself doing this and share the video with your admin.

By "processing" these emails in your inbox, we mean that you should start to become aware of why you're doing what you're doing with each email. What you'll realize is that you only receive a handful of "types" of emails and that you do the same things with each of those different types of emails each time. This means that once you become aware of each of these types of emails and how you handle them, they can then be processed and handed off to your admin. Below are some of the very common types of emails we've encountered and the processes we have our admin use to handle them.

1. SCHEDULING EMAILS

Definition:

Scheduling emails are any emails that require you to be involved in a meeting, whether internal or external, and in-person or as a conference call.

Example: "Hi Nate, do you have time today/this week for a call to discuss the Anderson acquisition?"

Rules:

- Prompt responses to scheduling emails from external sources is important to ensure Nate secures important meetings and calls.
- Nate receives many unsolicited/sales outreach emails that are not worth having calls or meetings with. If unsure, confirm with Nate before responding.
- Offer times that work for Nate.
- Be sure to clarify the meeting time zone and whether the meeting will be in-person or via a call and offer to send over the invite once the day/time/place is confirmed. Be sure to include any dial-in instructions for conference calls, and address and parking information for in-person meetings.
- Once the email is sent, snooze the email in Google Inbox for 3 days so that if the person doesn't respond, the email will show back up in Nate's inbox and you'll

be reminded to reach out to them again to set the meeting.

- ◦ *Example:* "Is there a best day/time this week for you to meet/have a call? Let me know what works best & I'll be happy to send over an invite."

2. INTRODUCTION EMAILS

Definition:

Introduction emails are any emails where either an internal team member or external contact introduces you to someone new.

Example: "Hi Dan, Hope you're all doing well! I wanted to introduce you to Nathan Pettijohn..."

Rules:

When people intro Nate via email, always thank them for the intro and **bcc** them on the reply.

- · If Nate is bcc'd on any email, never reply. It is generally a client or colleague giving visibility into an incoming introduction.
  - ◦ *Example:* "Thanks for the intro, Pat (bcc'd), and nice to meet you, Tim! ..."
- · Normally when Nate gets an intro email, the goal is

for Nate to setup a time to either meet in person or set an introductory call with that person, so reply with potential times to meet/talk with the new contact. Reply as Nate and in most cases, you'll treat these as scheduling emails (see above).

- Once the email is sent, snooze the email in your Google Inbox for 3 days (or the appropriate amount of time based on the context of the email) so that if the person doesn't respond, the email will show back up in Nate's inbox and you'll be reminded to reach out to them again to set the meeting.
- When Nate introduces himself in emails, use this text:

'Hi [x], Nice to e-meet. I would love to connect and learn more. Let me know what day(s)/time(s) work best for you and I'll be happy to send over an invite. Thanks and looking forward to connecting!'

Notes:

Feel free to add your template company overview or summary if you generally provide a full introduction of yourself. It may be more efficient for you to segment different types of introduction emails such as vendor intros and client intros each with their own template responses. Depending on what services your company provides, you should be able to utilize this same rule system based on the specifics of your inbox.

3. FOLLOW-UP EMAILS

Definition:

Follow-up emails are emails that you have sent to a prospective client or partner, with the intent of getting another meeting or some sort of action/response from the client/partner, that they have not responded to, and which have now resurfaced in your inbox.

Rules:

- Nate will handle these emails as they often need additional information in order to get the contact to respond.
- Leave these emails unread in the inbox so Nate knows that he needs to follow up on them.
  - *Example:* "Hi Doreen, I'm writing to follow-up on the below email. It would be great to secure a time for us to meet to discuss the research you are doing. Would 3:00 pm next Wednesday or 10:00 am next Thursday work for you? Thanks, and looking forward to connecting!"

4. EXPERTISE & OPINION EMAILS

Definition:

Expertise/opinion emails are emails where either internal/

external people are asking for your thoughts, opinions, or expertise on something.

Example: "Hi Nate, I just wrote this first draft of my new blog. What do you think?"

Rules:

- Do not reply to these emails unless Nate specifically asks you to with a specific response
- Leave these emails unread in Nate's inbox so that he knows he needs to respond to them
- Add task in Todoist and assign either to Nate or appropriate account manager

5. AUTOMATED SALESFORCE.COM EMAILS

Definition:

Salesforce.com emails are sent from Salesforce as updates that are happening on opportunities/accounts/contacts/ etc. that Nate or his team are associated with.

Rules:

- Read the email and if Nate is the owner of the opportunity, the email will tell you the next action you need to take

- Once you've taken the action in Salesforce that the email told you to take, archive the email
- If Nate isn't the owner of the opportunity, simply archive the email

6. VIP EMAILS

Rules are made to be broken, and our rules for automating and outsourcing email will be suspended when it comes to specific high-value clients and projects that require individualized attention.

Notice how many times in the guidelines below we have our admin send us a text, and also add a reminder to Todoist and assign the task to us there. Both appear as notifications on our phones. This is so we know right away when VIP Emails come in so we can make sure those don't slip between any cracks.

This is the one section of this book where it may not be possible for you to copy and paste our guidelines directly. Every business has different VIPs with different needs, so it is difficult to create a single template that works for everyone.

However, below we've suggested a few categories of VIP emails that may need processing. This is a real example from our business, regarding a specific client whose emails we do not respond to through automated or outsourced systems. (We've changed the client's names, her company's name, and the names of her staff members to protect their privacy.) When you design your own automated email processes, you'll need to tweak these rules somewhat for your own needs.

A. EMAILS DIRECTLY TO AND FROM VIPS

Definition:

VIP emails are any emails from **Jane Jackson or Bill Smith** to Nate. Only he will ever email VIPs or respond to their emails.

Example: "Hi Nate, what do you think of this blog? - **Jane**"

Rules: When listed VIPs send an email, text Nate immediately, add responding to the email to Todoist and assign to Nate.

- Do not reply to these emails unless Nate specifically asks you to with a specific response.
- Leave these emails unread in Nate's inbox so that he knows he needs to respond to them.
- Text Nate that Jane has emailed him, add to Todoist and assign to Nate.

B. EMAILS ABOUT VIPS

Definition:

Emails About VIPs emails are any emails that are sent to Nate about **Jane Jackson** or her business. The below rules and examples apply specifically to talent management, but the same basic principle can be applied to other industries as well. For example, a content marketing agency might have special rules for emails from freelancers about work for their biggest client. The exact guidelines must be adjusted for the specific situation.

Example: "Hi Nathan, John suggested I reach out to you regarding our new foundation, we would love to have **Jane Jackson** speak at our upcoming event or donate..."

Rules:

Prompt responses to **Jane Jackson** outreach emails from external sources is important to ensure **Jane Jackson** doesn't miss any opportunities.

- Thank them for reaching out and let them know their request will be reviewed to see if there is a fit.
  - *Example:* "Diana, thank you for thinking of **Jane**. Confirming I have received your note below. We will review on our end and let you know if there is a fit."

Once the email is sent, forward the email to **Jane's** publicist for his review and then add a task in Todoist assigned to Nate for him to also review opportunity.

C. VIP SCHEDULING EMAILS

Definition:

VIP Scheduling emails are any emails regarding scheduling meetings or phone calls with Jane Jackson. John Crawford is Jane Jackson's publicist. Emily Smith is her assistant. Once again, the below examples are specific to talent management; you should update with the scheduling rules that work for your business or industry.

Example: "Hi Nathan, the following interview with Jane on NPR has been confirmed for May 11th at 9am PST. – John Crawford"

Rules:

Any media request that comes in should be forwarded to John. He will help vet each opportunity and come back to us with times that work for the interview, shoot, or phone call. Emily will then confirm a time that works in **Jane**'s calendar. John will go back to the external contact to confirm the time, once he does that, he sends the confirmed time, location, and background info to Nate and Emily. These are always to then be sent to everyone from Nate's calendar.

Create calendar invite from Nate following scheduling email rules, (remove Google Hangout link, add address if applicable. For calls use Nate's dial in and add Eva to the invite.) Also invite **Jane**, Emily, John and the external contact (interviewer at NPR, for instance).

- Create reminder to send an email a week before the meeting and a day before the meeting to re-confirm and make sure everyone has confirmed.
  - *Example:* "Hi All, making sure we are all confirmed for the below dial-in on May 11th at 9am PST. Looking forward to it and please feel free to call me anytime to discuss."

7. PROJECT-SPECIFIC EMAILS

Definition: **Project-Specific** emails are any emails from anyone at our existing client **Widgets, Inc.** regarding their "x." Their account manager on our team is Isabella.

Example: "Hi Nate, please update our services to include x, y and z."

Rules:

- Do not reply to these emails unless Nate specifically asks you to with a specific response.
- Forward these emails to Isabella as she is the account manager.
- Add task in Todoist for Isabella to address the email.

QUICK TIP: VOICE MEMOS & EMAIL

The two of us live in Los Angeles (Nate) and New York City (Nic) and find we often come up with ideas and strategies when we are on the move, whether in an Uber or walking through NYC between meetings. The most efficient process we have found is adding voice memos to Todoist and assigning them to our admin, which allows us to have her draft emails or initiate specific post-meeting note sequences based on our dictation that we can then review and send later.

Any drafts can then become template emails on certain topics, saved in our CRM as a template and added to rules for sending as a response in the future. Saving your pitch or overview templates this way will save you and your admin hours of work each week.

Voice memos in Todoist are also crucial after meetings to record the takeaways and next steps (as you'll read about in a later section). Adding a voice memo that says, "Next step is us sending a specific document and case study to X client," gives your admin an easy way to draft those emails for you. Set specific times in your calendar when you are going to go through your emails to review and send these drafts, rather than having it become a never-ending task machine.

CALENDAR RULES

Google Calendar is a powerful tool when used correctly and efficiently. Here is the process our admin follows to take full advantage of GCal for all scheduling purposes. There are separate processes for scheduling work vs. personal events.

WORK SCHEDULING

1. Add all applicable attendees to the event.
2. Remove Hangouts unless I indicate to have one.
3. Add UberConference call info to every invite, even if they're in-person meetings.
   A. [UBERCONFERENCE DIAL-IN INFO GOES HERE]
4. Set 15-minute notifications.
5. Be sure to give appropriate amount of time between back to back in-person meetings.
6. Default meeting time should be 30 minutes unless otherwise indicated.
7. Breakfasts and lunches should be 1 hour unless otherwise indicated.
8. Add eva@voicera.com to all meetings whether they're in person or calls.
   A. Eva is an AI meeting assistant that listens to all my meetings so that I can recap them.
   B. You can go back in and search for keywords/ phrases see highlights or listen to the entire meeting.
   C. You'll receive debrief transcripts into my email inbox with my recap of the highlights from the meeting with next steps/action items.
9. Add address for all in-person meetings.

PERSONAL SCHEDULING

1. Add it to my work calendar so I don't have conflicts.
2. Set the event to private.

FOLLOW UPS

Following up efficiently after meetings is a critical piece of admin that requires clear guidelines. This document details what steps are included in following up on a meeting that Nate has had. You can adapt it for your own purposes.

FOLLOW UP EMAIL

Most meetings will require an email follow up to be sent from Nate to the person(s) that Nate met with.

After his meetings, Nate will add a to-do item in Todoist, assign it to his admin, and attach a voice note to it. In that note, he'll give you the high-level notes from the meeting as well as next steps and action items. From this voice note, you'll be able to compose a follow up email and complete any other applicable steps in the follow up process.

Below you'll find a sample follow up that Nate would send out which includes bulleted notes on their company, our company, and next steps/action items.

- Email title: always use the company or individual's name as the email title; this will make it very clear what the email is about and also very easy to go back and search for email chains
    - Example: *Brite //Acme Inc.* Follow Up
- Email body: use a very clean & organized structure. Leverage bullet points and breakout sections by content
    - what we learned about their company on the call as it pertains to our conversation
    - what they learned about our company as it pertains to our conversation
    - next steps/action items
    - Ask if we missed or misheard any information
- Example: see sample email below in blue
- Once you've sent the email, be sure to snooze the email using Google Inbox for the appropriate amount of time so that if the person doesn't reply to the email or we're supposed to follow up on it, we don't miss it.
    - Example: The client says, "Check back in with us in 3 weeks and we should have more information on when we can launch the campaigns." You'd want to compose the follow up email, send it, then snooze that email for 3 weeks then send another follow up to check in then.

SAMPLE FOLLOW-UP EMAIL

Hey Chad,

Hope your week is off to a great start! I just wanted to follow up quickly on a few notes and action items from our call last week:

Acme Inc. Notes:

- Acme's vision/mission:
- Acme's goals:
- Acme's top priority right now:
- Acme's biggest challenge right now:

Brite Overview:

- How Brite can help Acme:
- Why Brite is right for the job:

Next Steps & Action Items

- Insert description of next steps here, formatted as a bulleted list
- Be sure to include the goals these next steps are going to achieve

Does that sound like we got everything?

We're really looking forward to working with you guys!

ADDING ACTION ITEMS IN TODOIST

- If there are action items from this meeting, add them to Todoist and assign them either to yourself or to Nate and add any applicable due dates to the action items

UPDATING SALESFORCE.COM OPPORTUNITY

- Once you've done the prior steps, then you should update the opportunity this follow up is related to in Salesforce, if it exists.

CONCLUSION

Administrative work is a bit like empty calories: it can make you feel as though your day is full and productive, but in reality, it's just slowing you down, making you tired, and keeping you from achieving your best results.

While sending emails, updating calendars, and ticking boxes can give you that immediate sense of getting things done, you're really just doing the same tasks over and over, and blocking yourself from getting in the whitespace hours you need to produce creative, transformative ideas, products, and businesses.

That whitespace—those periods of time where you're entirely free from the drudgery of syncing schedules and the tyranny of inboxes and menial to-dos—is where your work truly lies. It's where you'll generate real breakthroughs, real societal contributions, and real wealth. No one has ever gained wealth, power, or fame because they were excellent at admin work.

Hopefully the examples above are easy for most readers to implement into their daily workflow, yielding an immediate increase in whitespace. At the very least, we hope these templates themselves can serve as a springboard to thinking about how you can document, template-ize and delegate more of your own admin tasks. Remember that these are merely tools and confusing input with output doesn't drive growth. There are only 24 hours in the day, no matter how successful you are.

Documenting and delegating your processes forces you to simplify your steps and language. In the same vein of 'Keep it simple, stupid,' delegating work to an admin makes you be very precise. Thinking your processes through with the goal of easy repeatability is a helpful exercise in itself, because it helps you refine those processes while forcing you to document, delegate and automate.

It's worth noting that there is such a thing as too much automation. There are scheduling tools that some people use to email a public link where you can book a time to speak with them. That just tells us that their time isn't valuable at all, and they probably aren't worth scheduling a call with. There are smart ways to utilize tools, just as there are many ways to actually hinder your personal brand by using the right tools in the wrong ways. The best way to eat an elephant is one bite at a time, so just take step one and delegate your inbox and calendar. Don't add more tools just for the sake of having more tools.

We do plan to cover other processes besides email and scheduling, but that will have to wait for other books. For now, we will just note that it is worth using this methodology of template responses and an admin for other repeatable processes like data entry, lead generation, drip campaigns or managing your social media.

In running social media accounts for our clients for instance, we have processes for messages there based on template responses. Our employees send ten direct messages a day to CEOs from Nate's personal Instagram based on copy he wrote, and they handle all the commenting, liking and following. Sometimes you have to decide that looking at your phone isn't moving you forward. That can also mean not participating in social media at all, but for us it's a matter of practicing what we preach.

See your email and calendar as step one in a road to letting go of the trivial. All of these processes can move a company forward, but that doesn't mean that you personally need to be micromanaging everything.

Our work may be specific to digital strategy and marketing, but the more you document and delegate in any business, the less you are micromanaging. That is usually a good thing. Send a message on LinkedIn, and it gets put in a funnel with specific responses based on the topic that one of our employees will respond with. Forward movement is being made in a professional and timely manner, why should it matter that it lacks personal or emotional flair?

If you are motivated to build your organization, you won't see these tips as a way to suddenly start spending all your days at the golf course. Instead, you can save hours out of your day by not doing admin work and focus instead on projects that you are passionate about. We still devote many hours of our days to work, but we are now able to hone in and focus our time on the work that we think will drive the most return rather than work that just makes us feel like we're being productive.

A solid, automated, outsourced administrative system will save you valuable time and energy, which you can then use to create real value for your company. By implementing these tools and systems, you will find yourself with dozens of hours of whitespace time that you previously did not have. You can fill that time with more productive, value-generating activities including ideation, deep-thinking, and creative play.

Your mind and business may be special, but your inbox and your schedule don't need to be; free yourself from the cycle of small tasks and embrace your time and energy as a creator and knowledge worker.

ABOUT THE
AUTHORS

NIC DE CASTRO and **NATHAN PETTIJOHN** both work with Strike Social and met via their CEO Patrick McKenna. Strike Social is the 17th fastest growing company in the United States according to *Inc.* magazine.

Nic De Castro is a sales leader in the marketing technology industry with a breadth of experience both building businesses and selling products to the largest advertisers on the planet. He's lived in Boston, LA, Chicago, NYC, SF, Boulder, & Bozeman and has nearly broken 1M miles for work travel, but has been fortunate to sneak quite a bit of fun into those miles over the years. Nic is VP of Strategic Partnerships at Strike Social.

Nathan Pettijohn is a talent manager, producer, and growth hacker. In 2011, Nathan founded Cordurouy, where he now serves as CEO. Cordurouy leads digital strategy for numerous brands and influencers. As a talent manager, Nathan represents business innovators such as Janice Bryant Howroyd (Founder and CEO, The ActOne Group). He is also a contributing writer for Forbes on topics relating to what business leaders need to know about innovations in media and digital strategy.

APPENDIX

UPWORK JOB POSTING FOR ADMIN

UpWork Job description:

I'm looking for a skilled, articulate, admin to support me in my new VP job at an advertising company. Things that will be covered by this role will be: managing my email inbox, scheduling, assisting in client follow up, salesforce. com updating, etc.

UpWork Interview Questions:

You will be asked to answer the following questions when submitting a proposal:

1. Why are you freelancing? What's your ability to set up new systems for work?
2. Do you have any questions about the job description?
3. What past project or job have you had that is most like this one and why?

Keep your account information in one place for administrative ease.

G SUITE
Username:

Password:

UBERCONFERENCE
Conference Line:

Pin Number:

VOICERA
Username:

Password:

NIMBLE

Username:

Password:

TODOIST

Username:

Password:

CRYSTAL

Username:

Password:

DETECTIVE

Username:

Password:

LOOM

Username:

Password:

Mobile phone:

Phone number:

Voicemail PIN:

Made in the USA
San Bernardino, CA
19 July 2018